TABLE OF CO

CATEGORY CRAZE

Encourage students to develop their categorizing skills in this fun fast-paced game.

WHAT YOU NEED:

No materials needed.

WHAT YOU DO:

1. Explain to the students that a category is a group or set of things, people, or actions that are classified together because of common characteristics. Give an example of a category and a word that belongs in it. For example, the category pets and the word dog.

2. Arrange the class into two teams. As students participate and name a word for the category they receive points for their team. Keep a tally score on the chalkboard.

3. Call out a new category when there are no more words offered by either team.

4. Set a time limit on the game and declare the winning team at the conclusion.

SAMPLE CATEGORIES:

• authors	• sports
• colours	• games
• animals	• toys
• plants	• fruits
• cities	• names
• shoes	• dwellings
• vegetables	• fish
• occupations	• birds
• vegetables	• languages
• countries	• transportation

Chalkboard Publishing © 2008

NEWSLETTER

What did we do in school today?

MONDAY

TUESDAY

WEDNESDAY

THURSDAY

FRIDAY

NOTES

PROUD TO BE CANADIAN!

List ten reasons why you are proud to be Canadian.

1.	
2.	
3.	
4.	
5.	
6.	
7.	
8.	
9.	
10.	

COMMON PROVERBS AND SAYINGS

Challenge students' thinking! As a group discussion or as an individual writing activity ask students to explain the meaning of the following proverbs and sayings. Can students relate these common proverbs and sayings to their everyday life? If so, have students give examples.

1. Actions speak louder than words.

2. A fool and his money are soon parted.

3. All good things must come to an end.

4. All is not gold that glitters.

5. An apple a day, keeps the doctor away.

6. An elephant never forgets.

7. As you make your bed, so you must lie in it.

8. The bark is worse than the bite.

9. Beauty is only skin deep.

10. Better safe than sorry.

11. Business before pleasure.

12. Do not bite off more than you can chew.

13. Don't put your eggs all in one basket.

14. Don't count your chickens before they hatch.

15. Don't cut off your nose to spite your face.

16. Finders keepers.

17. Forgive and forget.

18. Good news travels fast.

19. Have a place for everything, and everything has a place.

20. Honesty is the best policy.

21. It's easier said than done.

22. Knowledge is power.

23. Last but not least.

24. Let bygones be bygones.

25. Look before you leap.

26. Out of the frying pan and into the fire.

27. A penny saved is a penny earned.

28. Birds of a feather flock together.

COMMON PROVERBS AND SAYINGS

29. Money doesn't grow on trees.

30. Paddle your own canoe.

31. Practice what you preach.

32. The early bird catches the worm.

33. The pot calls the kettle black.

34. The proof of the pudding is in the eating.

35. The proud hate pride—in others.

36. The race is not always to the swift, nor the battle to the strong.

37. The rolling stone gathers no moss.

38. The walls have ears.

39. There are other fish in the sea.

40. There are two sides to every story.

41. There is no time like the present.

42. There's no place like home.

43. They also serve who only stand and wait.

44. Throw mud and some of it will stick.

45. Time is money.

46. To err is human, to forgive divine.

47. To the pure all things are pure.

48. Tomorrow never comes.

49. Too many cooks spoil the broth.

50. Too much curiosity killed the cat.

51. Truth is stranger than fiction.

52. Two can live cheaper than one.

53. Two heads are better than one.

54. Two is company, three is a crowd.

55. Two wrongs don't make a right.

56. United we stand, divided we fall.

57. Virtue is its own reward.

58. Walk your talk.

59. Waste not, want not.

60. Watch your step.

61. We are what we eat.

COMMON PROVERBS AND SAYINGS

62. We have nothing to fear but fear itself.

63. We live and learn.

64. We must stoop to conquer.

65. We're here today and gone tomorrow.

66. Well begun is half done.

67. What is sauce for the goose is sauce for the gander.

68. What we do in haste we repent at leisure.

69. What will be, will be.

70. What's worth doing is worth doing well.

71. Whatever is worth doing at all is worth doing well.

72. When angry, count to ten.

73. When in doubt, leave it out.

74. When one door shuts, another opens.

75. When the blind lead the blind they all fall into the ditch.

76. When the cat is away the mice will play.

77. When the night is darkest the dawn is nearest.

78. Where there is a will there is a way.

79. Where there is smoke, there is fire.

80. You can catch more flies with honey than with vinegar.

81. You can lead a horse to water, but you can't make him drink.

82. You can't eat your cake and have it too.

83. You can't judge a book by its cover.

84. You can't make an omelette without breaking eggs.

85. You can't teach an old dog new tricks.

86. You can't win them all.

87. You win some, you lose some.

88. You never know what you can do until you try.

89. You never miss the water until the well runs dry.

90. You're never too old to learn.

100 OF CANADA'S WILDLIFE

Here are some excellent websites where you can find out about Canada's wildlife.

- www.hww.ca
- www.canadianfauna.com

MAMMALS

1.	Arctic Fox	19.	Moose
2.	Atlantic walrus	20.	Mountain Goat
3.	Bats	21.	Mountain Sheep
4.	Beaver	22.	Muskox
5.	Beluga whale	23.	Muskrat
6.	Black Bear	24.	North American Bison
7.	Bowhead whale	25.	North American Elk
8.	Canada Lynx	26.	Polar Bear
9.	Caribou	27.	Porcupine
10.	Chipmunk	28.	Raccoon
11.	Cougar	29.	Red Fox
12.	Coyote	30.	Snowshoe Hare
13.	Eastern Grey Squirrel	31.	Striped Skunk
14.	Grizzly	32.	Swift Fox
15.	Harbour porpoise	33.	White-tailed Deer
16.	Killer whale	34.	Wolf
17.	Lemmings	35.	Wolverine
18.	Marten	36.	Woodchuck

AMPHIBIANS AND REPTILES

37.	Wood Frog	40.	Red-Legged Frog
38.	Leatherback Seaturtle	41.	Boreal Chorus Frog
39.	Western Garter Snake	42.	Horned Lizard

BIRDS

43.	American Black Duck	61.	Great Blue Heron	79.	Purple Martin
44.	American Goldfinch	62.	Great Horned Owl	80.	Red-breasted Nuthatch
45.	American Robin	63.	Greater Snow Goose	81.	Redhead
46.	Arctic Tern	64.	Harlequin Duck	82.	Ring-billed Gull
47.	Atlantic Puffin	65.	Herring Gull	83.	Roseate Tern
48.	Bald Eagle	66.	Killdeer	84.	Ruby-throated Hummingbird
49.	Bicknell's Thrush	67.	Lesser Snow Goose	85.	Ruffed Grouse
50.	Black-capped Chickadee	68.	Loggerhead Shrike	86.	Seabirds
51.	Blue Jay	69.	Loons	87.	Semipalmated Sandpiper
52.	Bufflehead	70.	Mallard	88.	Sharp-shinned Hawk, Cooper's Hawk, and Northern Goshawk
53.	Burrowing Owl	71.	Marbled Murrelet	89.	Shorebirds
54.	Canada Goose	72.	Mountain Bluebird	90.	Snowy Owl
55.	Canvasback	73.	Murres	91.	Trumpeter Swan
56.	Cassin's Auklet	74.	Northern Gannet	92.	Tundra Swan
57.	Common Eider	75.	Osprey	93.	Whooping Crane
58.	Downy Woodpecker	76.	Peregrine Falcon	94.	Wild Turkey
59.	Evening Grosbeak	77.	Piping Plover	95.	Wood Duck
60.	Gray Jay	78.	Ptarmigan		

FISH

96.	Atlantic Whitefish	99.	Salmon
97.	Arctic Grayling	100.	Rainbow Trout
98.	Northern Pike		

CANADIAN WILDLIFE REPORT

Name of Animal _____

Circle One: **Mammal**   **Reptile**   **Amphibian**   **Fish**   **Bird**

What does it look like?	
Where is its habitat?	
What does it eat?	
What are its special features?	
Interesting Fact	
Interesting Fact	
Interesting Fact	

ACROSTIC POEM

Acrostic poems are poems in which the first letter of each line forms a word or phrase (vertically). An acrostic poem can describe the subject or even tell a brief story about it.

SENSATIONAL SIMILES

A *simile* is a phrase that contains the word *"like"* or *"as"* to make a comparison between two different things.

For example: David was as hungry as a bear!

Write some of your own similies.

1 _____

2 _____

3 _____

4 _____

5 _____

6 _____

7 _____

8 _____

9 _____

10 _____

AMAZING ALLITERATIONS

Alliterations are sentences or phrases that contain words that repeat the same beginning word sound.

For example: Alfred alligator always acts annoyingly

Create some of your own examples of alliterations below.

1 _____

2 _____

3 _____

4 _____

5 _____

6 _____

7 _____

8 _____

9 _____

10 _____

Mountie: _____

Beaver: _____

Mountie: _____

Beaver: _____

Mountie: _____

Beaver: _____

Mountie: _____

Beaver: _____

NIAGARA FALLS

Niagara Falls, Ontario is world famous! Niagara Falls is on the Niagara River and is fifty-two metres tall. There are two ways to see Niagara Falls up close. The first way is to go "under the falls" through a tunnel that takes visitors to a sightseeing point near the falls. The second way is to take a ride on the Maid of the Mist boat, which carries visitors close to the falls.

- Colour Niagara Falls.
- Draw the Maid of the Mist boat at the bottom of the falls.

BRAIN STRETCH

Would you rather go under the falls or take a ride on the Maid of the Mist boat? Explain your thinking.

A WORD SEARCH ABOUT

Create a word search and share it with your classmates.

(empty word search grid)

AY i ZB **WORD** LIST C J R U X

WORD LIST

(empty word list table)

Chalkboard Publishing © 2008

WANTED!

Who or what?

_____

Last seen?

_____

_____

Description?

_____

_____

Wanted for?

_____

_____

Reward?

_____

DESCRIBE A CHARACTER

Book Title: _____

Author: _____

Character Name: _____

Character Trait:

Explain Your Thinking:

Character Trait:

Explain Your Thinking:

STORY WRITING WORKSHOP

Story Title _____

BEGINNING

- [ ] I wrote an attention grabbing first sentence.
- [ ] I introduced the main character.
- [ ] I wrote about where the story takes place.

_____

_____

_____

_____

_____

_____

_____

_____

- [ ] I checked for capitals and periods.   - [ ] I added adjectives.

STORY WRITING WORKSHOP

Story Title _____

MIDDLE

☐ **I explained the problem in the story.**

_____

_____

_____

_____

_____

_____

_____

_____

_____

_____

_____

☐ **I checked for capitals and periods.**   ☐ **I added adjectives.**

STORY WRITING WORKSHOP

Story Title _____

EVENTS

☐ I wrote about events that happen in the story before the problem is solved.

Event 1

_____

_____

_____

_____

Event 2

_____

_____

_____

_____

☐ I checked for capitals and periods.　　☐ I added adjectives.　　☐ I explained each event.

STORY WRITING WORKSHOP

Story Title _____

ENDING

☐ **I explained how the problem was solved.**

_____

_____

_____

_____

_____

_____

_____

_____

_____

_____

☐ **I checked for capitals and periods.**   ☐ **I added adjectives.**

SUPER STORY RETELL

Read a story. Retell what happened in the story in your own words.

Story Title _____

BEGINNING

_____

_____

_____

_____

_____

_____

SUPER STORY RETELL

Read a story. Retell what happened in the story in your own words.

Story Title _____

MIDDLE

_____

_____

_____

_____

_____

_____

_____

SUPER STORY RETELL

Read a story. Retell what happened in the story in your own words.

Story Title _____

END

_____

_____

_____

_____

_____

_____

COMPARISON CHART

Information

Comparing...

Information

Comparing...

Comparing...

ROYAL CANADIAN MOUNTED POLICE

"We always get our man!"

COLOUR THE FOLLOWING:

COAT: bright red
HAT: tan with a black band
BOOTS: brown
BELT: black
BUTTONS: yellow
PANTS: black with yellow stripes

Add and colour a background.

What do you think are the characteristics of a "mountie"?

_____

_____

_____

_____

_____

OGOPOGO

Ogopogo is famous! Some people believe that Ogopogo lives in the waters of British Columbia. Do you think Ogopogo is real? Explain your ideas!

_____

_____

_____

_____

_____

_____

_____

OGOPOGO ADVENTURE

Write ideas for your story in this story planner.

Where will the adventure take place?

Who will be in the adventure?

How does the adventure begin?

What happens in the adventure?

How does the adventure end?

Book Title	Author	Would you recommend this book?

A VENN DIAGRAM ABOUT

_____

_____   _____

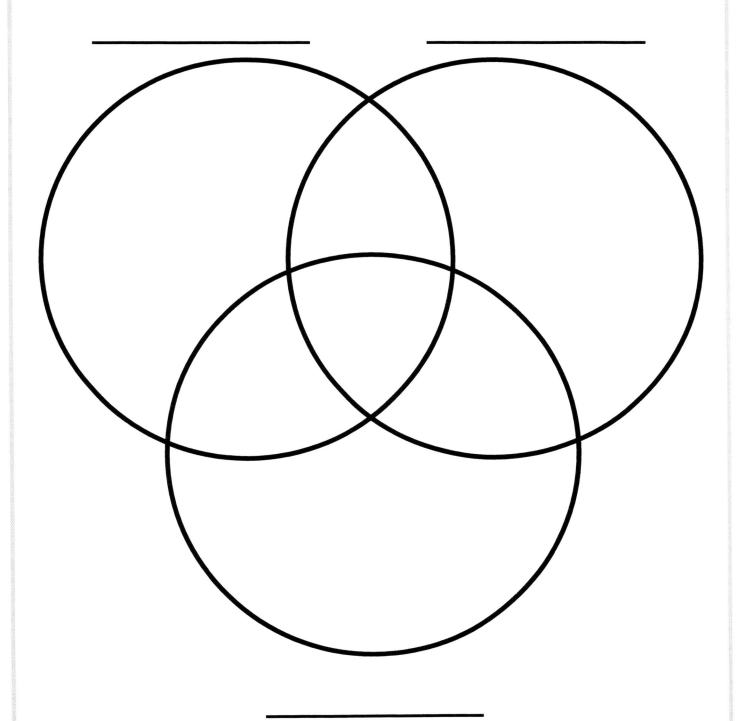

_____

A VENN DIAGRAM ABOUT

_____

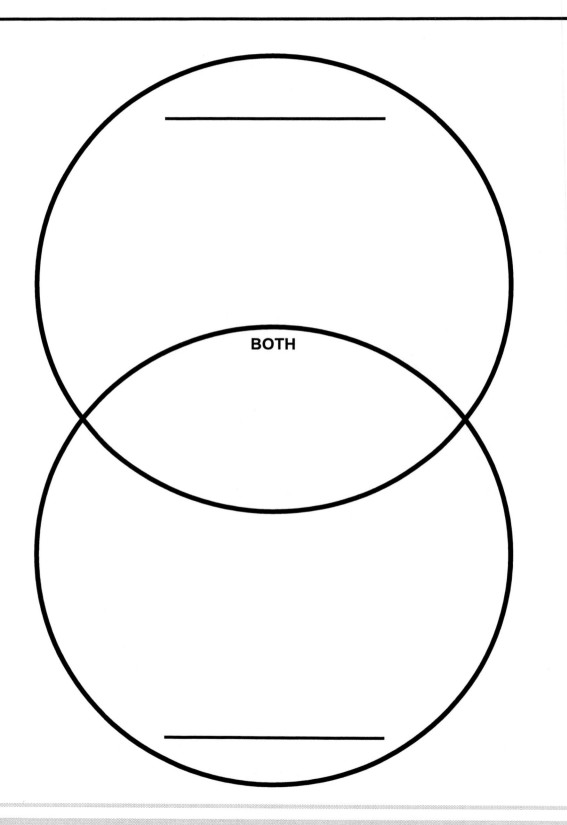

_____

BOTH

_____

A WEB ABOUT

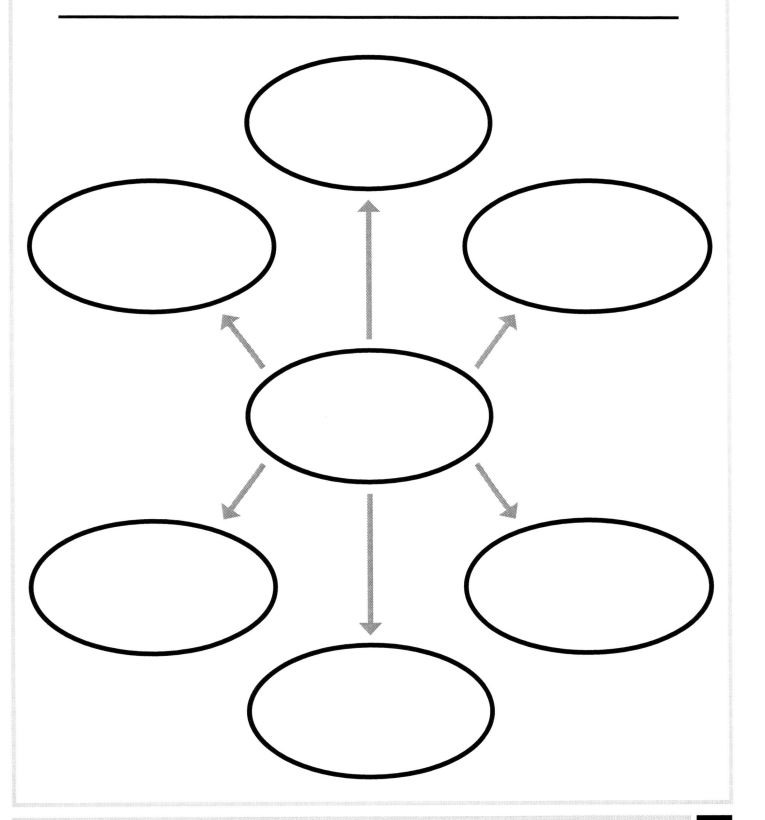

WOULD YOU RATHER...?

Use these fun questions as a springboard for discussion or for journal writing. Challenge students to come up with their own questions.

1. Would you rather live in the ocean or in space? Tell why.

2. Would you rather visit a volcano or the rainforest? Tell why.

3. Would you rather be as tiny as a mouse or as big as a dinosaur? Tell why.

4. Would you rather eat vegetables or fruit? Tell why.

5. Would you rather visit the doctor or the dentist? Tell why.

6. Would you rather have snowy weather or sunny and warm weather? Tell why.

7. Would you rather be a child or a grown up? Tell why.

8. Would you rather live in the city or the country? Tell why.

9. Would you rather play outside or play on the computer? Tell why.

11. Would you rather take a trip by a train or by an airplane? Tell why.

12. Would you rather have a pet cat or dog? Tell why.

13. Would you rather do math or reading? Tell why.

14. Would you rather be the youngest in your family or the oldest? Tell why.

15. Would you rather be a fish or a bird? Tell why.

16. Would you rather be able to fly or to have super strength? Tell why.

PERSONAL POSTCARD

Write a postcard to a friend.

Front of Postcard:

Back of Postcard:

To:

FACT OR OPINION

Topic

Fact

Opinion

DRAW A MAP

A map is a flat drawing of a place. Choose a place and draw a map. Create a legend that includes symbols to help people find things on your map.

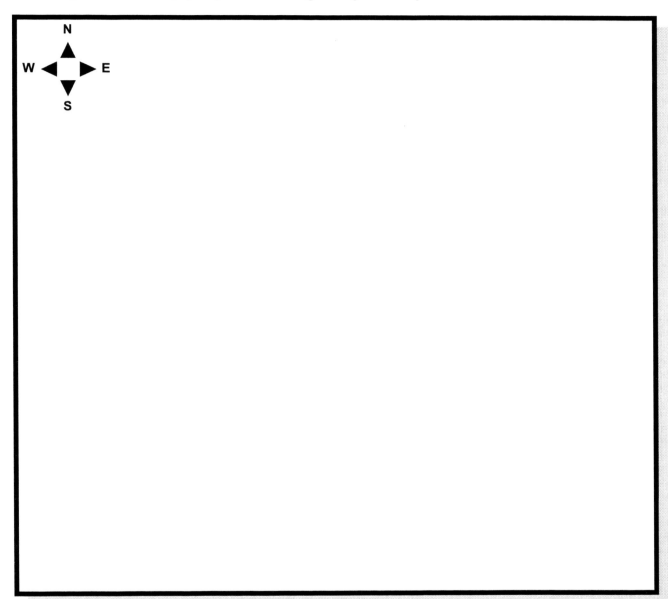

LEGEND

CRAZY COLOURING IDEAS

As a great time filler, have children practice their fine motor skills using different media to colour colouring pages or simple geometric shapes.

Colour a colouring page or large geometric shapes:

- on different surfaces such as sand paper to create interesting textures

- alternating heavy and light strokes

- using only primary colours

- using only secondary colours

- using different shades of the same colour

- with different colours of chalk and setting it with hair spray

- using pastels

- using watercolours

- vertical lines

- horizontal lines

Fill in sections of a colouring page or geometric shape using:

- different colours of plastiscene

- tiny bits of torn construction paper

- mixed media

- different colours of thick yarn

- different patterns

- cotton swab dots

Create a stamp.

Write about your stamp:

_____

_____

DIRECT DRAW

Encourage students to think of art as the personal interpretation of ideas. This is a quick art activity that demonstrates for students how, with the same directions, each student's execution of those directions is unique. At the end of the activity, collect all of the students' art and create a wonderful display of abstract art based on shape, colour and line.

WHAT YOU NEED:

- piece of square paper
- colouring materials

WHAT YOU DO:

1. Instruct students to follow the directions in order to complete a piece of art.

2. Take a survey of the class to predict if they think all of students' artwork will look the same if everyone follows the same directions.

3. Next call out directions such as the following:
   - draw a thin line across the page.
   - draw a thick line across the page.
   - draw a circle anywhere on your paper.
   - draw a triangle somewhere on your paper.
   - directions of your choice that will reinforce art vocabulary.

4. Once the directions are called out, have students compare their artwork with a partner, focusing on how the art pieces are the same or different.

5. Display the students' artwork as a combined piece of group art.

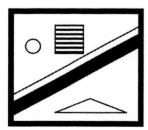 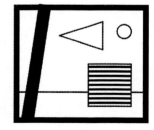 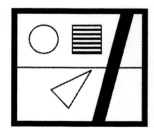 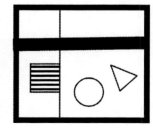

GIANT CLASS PUZZLE

Design a giant class puzzle! Give each person in the class a puzzle piece to create something to add to a giant class puzzle composition. Some ideas for the giant class puzzle include:

- each puzzle piece is a picture that fits into a class theme
- each puzzle piece is a research report on the same topic
- each puzzle piece is a poem to create a class anthology

GIANT CLASS PUZZLE

GIANT CLASS PUZZLE

DRAW A PORTRAIT

Draw a portrait of a family member, friend, or pet .

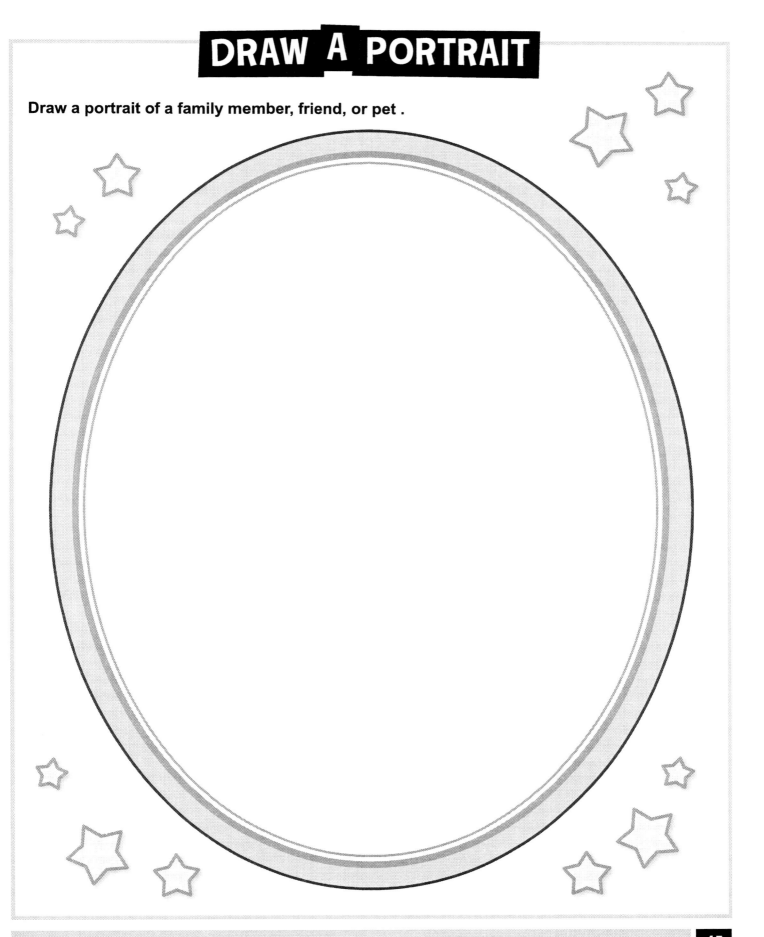

Design your own Canadian $100 bill.

This is what a real $100 bill looks like!

100

BANK OF CANADA • BANQUE DU CANADA

CANADA
CENT • ONE HUNDRED
DOLLARS

100

Write about your $100 bill:

_____

_____

_____

_____

DESIGN YOUR OWN $1.00 COIN

Design your own Canadian $1.00 coin.

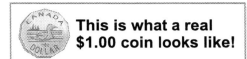
This is what a real $1.00 coin looks like!

The nickname for the Canadian $1.00 coin is the loonie. What is the nickname of your $1.00 coin and why?

_____

_____

CRAZY CHECKERS

Use this game board and cut out the game pieces to play a game of checkers.

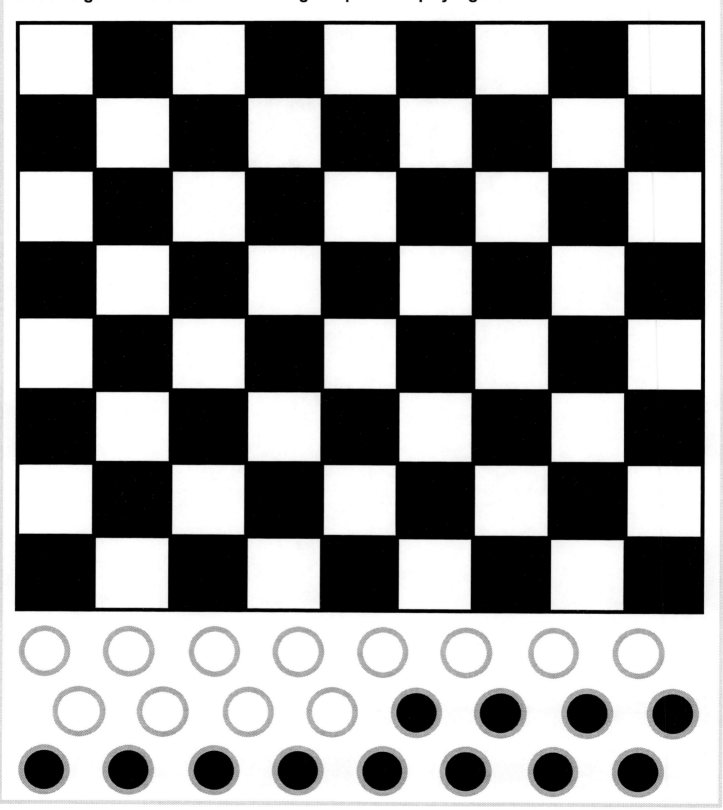

Create your own personal flag.

COMMUNITY COLLAGE

Make a collage about your community! Look through magazines, brochures, or newspapers to find people, places, things or words that remind you of your community. Cut and paste these pictures into a collage in the space below.

Write about your community.

_____

_____

Chalkboard Publishing © 2008

INUKSHUK

An Inukshuk is a stone marker to show the way. Inukshuk means "expressing joy." Make your own Inukshuk by tearing and pasting grey construction paper.

Get three X's in a row (horizontal, vertical, or diagonal) before your partner gets three O's in a row.

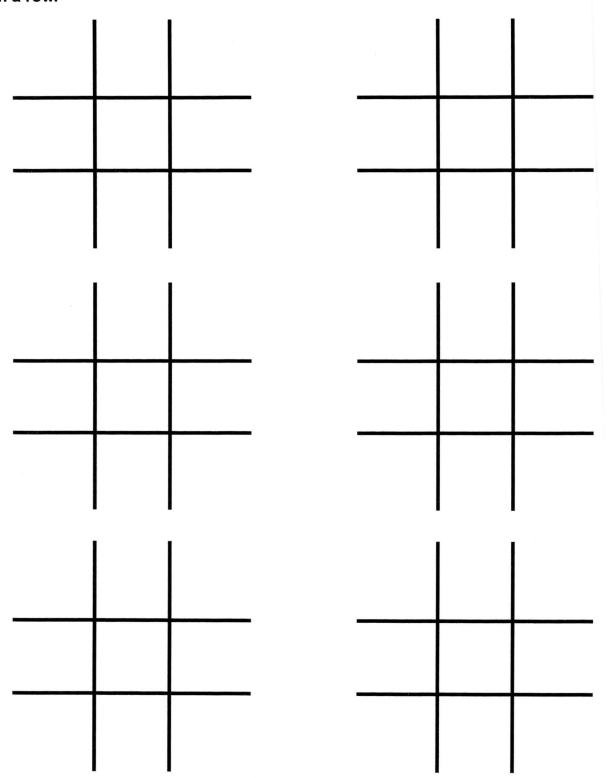

MYSTERY MAZE

Help the mouse get to the cheese!

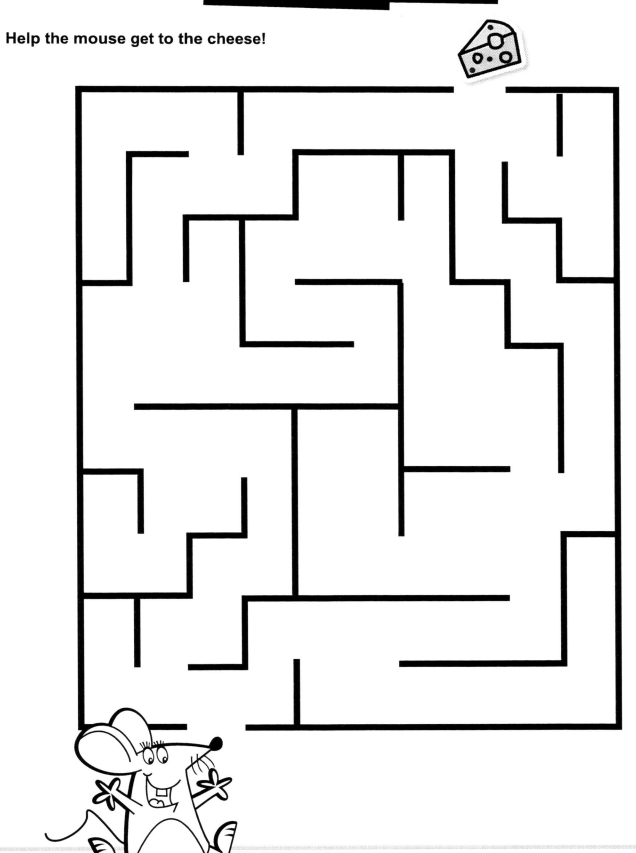

RACE TO 100

Roll the dice! Challenge your partner to see who can reach 100 first!

WHAT YOU NEED:

base ten pieces	a pair of dice	place value sheet

WHAT YOU DO:

1. Player 1 rolls the dice.

2. Player 1 counts out that number of "ones" and puts it on their place value sheet in the "ones" column.

3. Player 2 rolls the dice.

4. Player 2 counts out that number of "ones" and puts it on their place value sheet in the "ones" column.

5. Players regroup the "ones" to "tens" whenever possible.

6. The first player to regroup their "tens" to 100 wins!

RACE TO 100

1's	
10's	
100's	

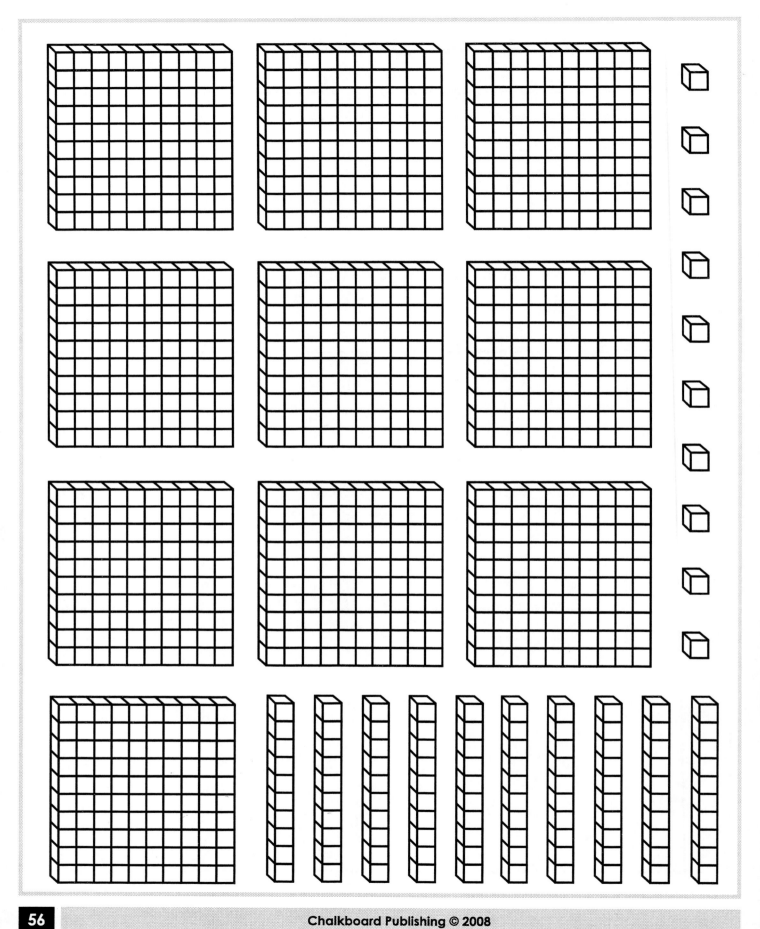

TERRIFIC TANGRAMS

A tangram is an ancient Chinese puzzle made from seven geometric shapes. The objective is to form a specific shape with these seven pieces.

1. Carefully cut out the tangram shapes below.

2. Use the tangram shapes to construct an animal, person or thing. Your new shape design must contain all the pieces, which may not overlap.

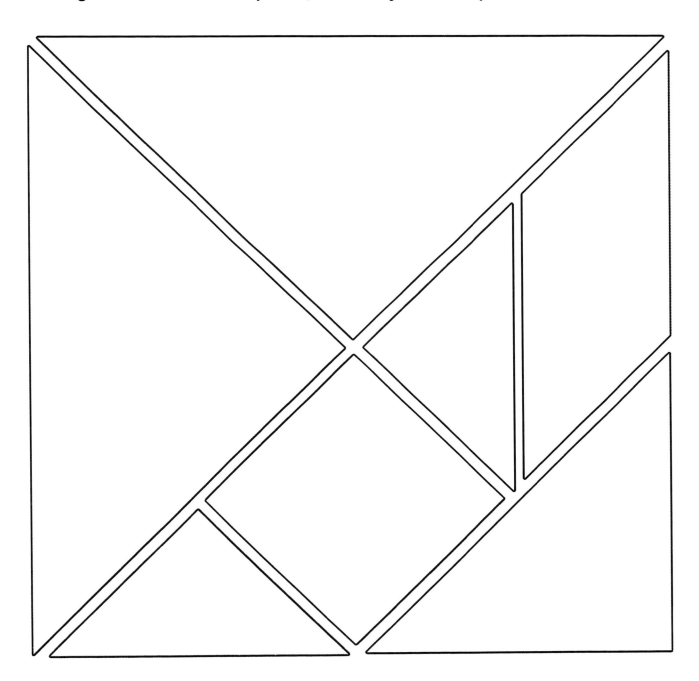

See how many of these tangram animal puzzles you can solve.

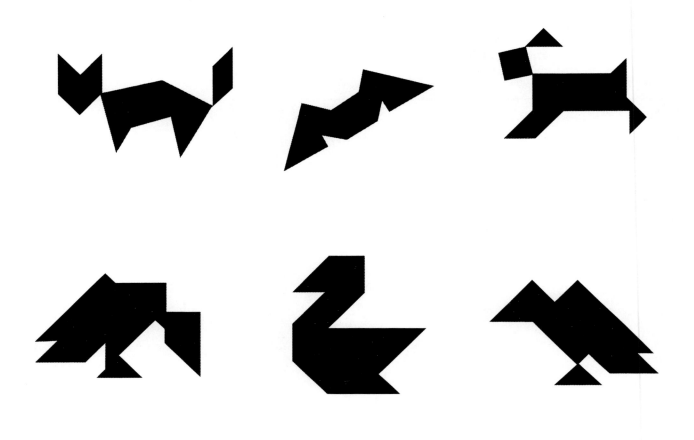

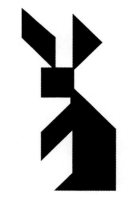

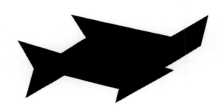

SECRET CODE

Create a message using this secret code.

A	B	C	D	E
#	$	≡	◎	☾

F	G	H	I	J
☼	◇	((	△	@

K	L	M	N	O
♡	⇧	//	=	●

P	Q	R	S	T
Ψ	⊕	⊠	¢	«

U	V	W	X	Y
‡	▭	%	∧	*

Z
+

CREATE YOUR OWN SECRET CODE

Create symbols for each letter of the alphabet to invent your secret code.
Write a message.

A	B	C	D	E
F	G	H	I	J
K	L	M	N	O
P	Q	R	S	T
U	V	W	X	Y
Z				

SUPER SHAPE CONCENTRATION

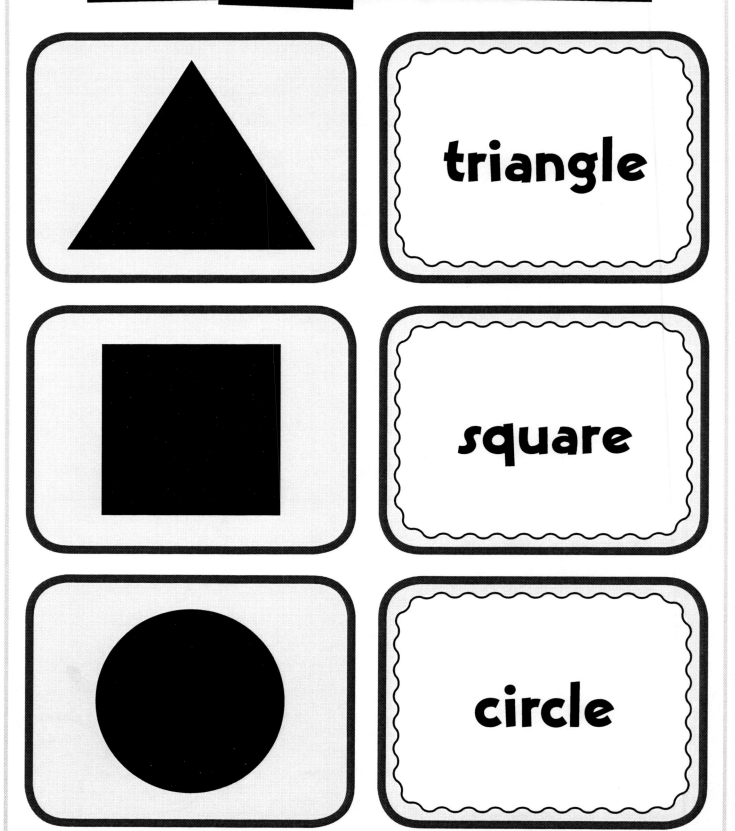

triangle

square

circle

SUPER SHAPE CONCENTRATION

rectangle

pentagon

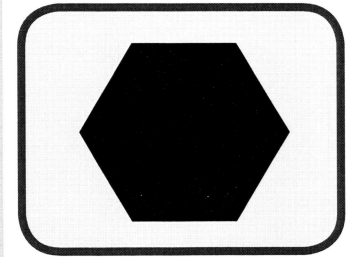

hexagon

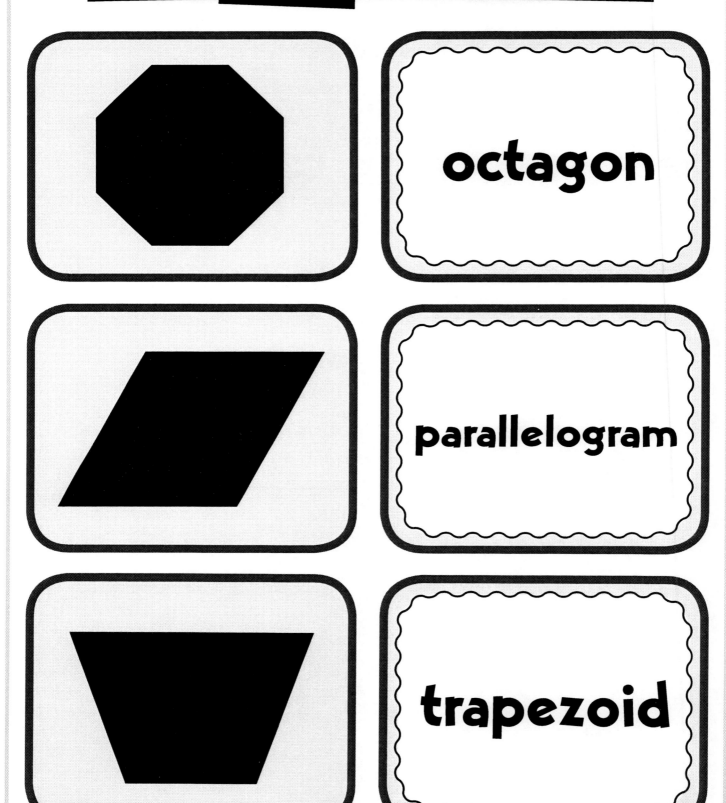

octagon

parallelogram

trapezoid

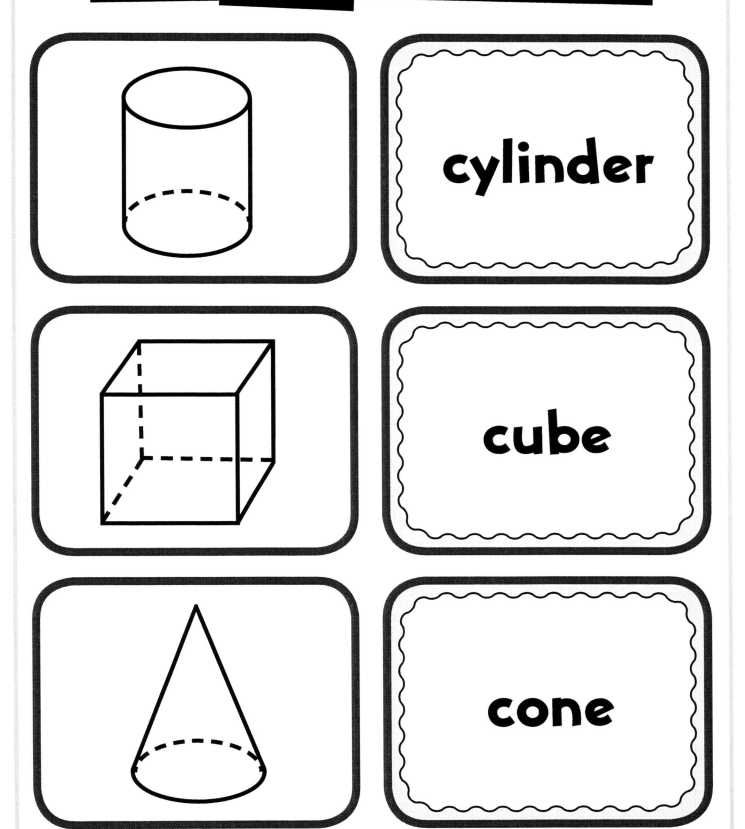

cylinder

cube

cone

SUPER SHAPE CONCENTRATION

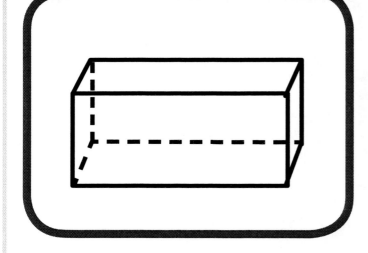

rectangular prism

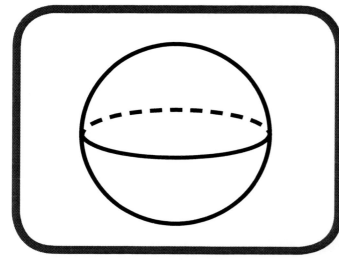

sphere

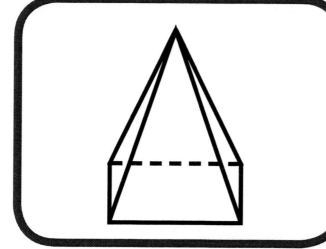

pyramid

COUNTING CHANGE

How many coins do you need to show each amount of money? Answers will vary.

	1¢	5¢	10¢	25¢
23¢				
67¢				
88¢				
35¢				
46¢				
92¢				
80¢				
71¢				
56¢				
14¢				
50¢				

CREATE A BOARD GAME

Create your own board game! Base your game on a theme you are studying in class or something in which you are interested.

WHAT YOU NEED:

- game board black line master
- colouring materials
- dice
- scissors
- glue
- construction paper

WHAT YOU DO:

1. Choose a theme for your game.
2. Glue the two game board blackline masters onto construction paper to create the game board.
3. Decorate your game board to make it colourful and eyecatching.
4. Create game cards with questions for players to answer so that they can move along in the game.
5. Cut small figures out of paper use as game pieces or use other materials that are available.
6. Write directions on how to play your game.
7. Play your game!

GAME CARD IDEAS:

- math questions
- true or false
- answer the question

GAME BOARD CARDS

Create game cards for your board game.

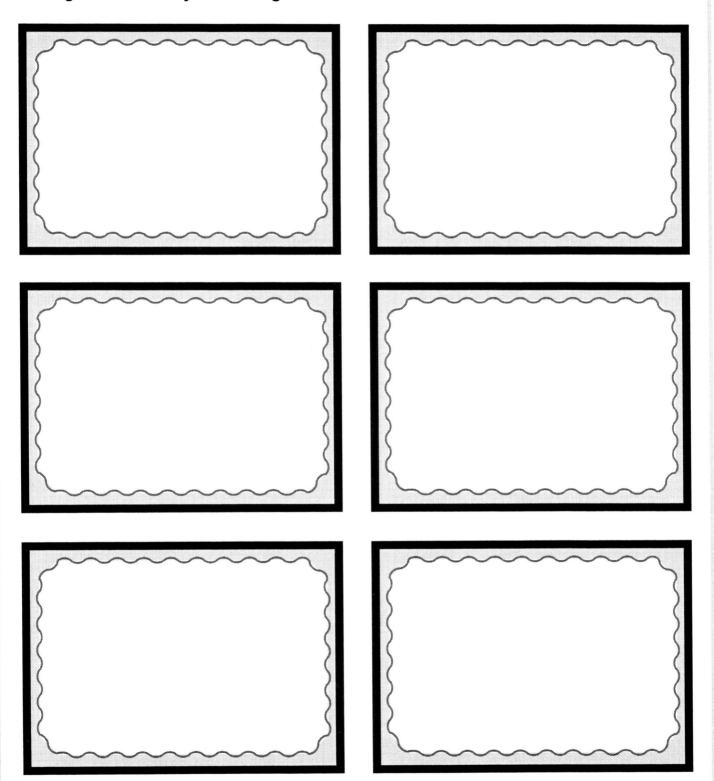

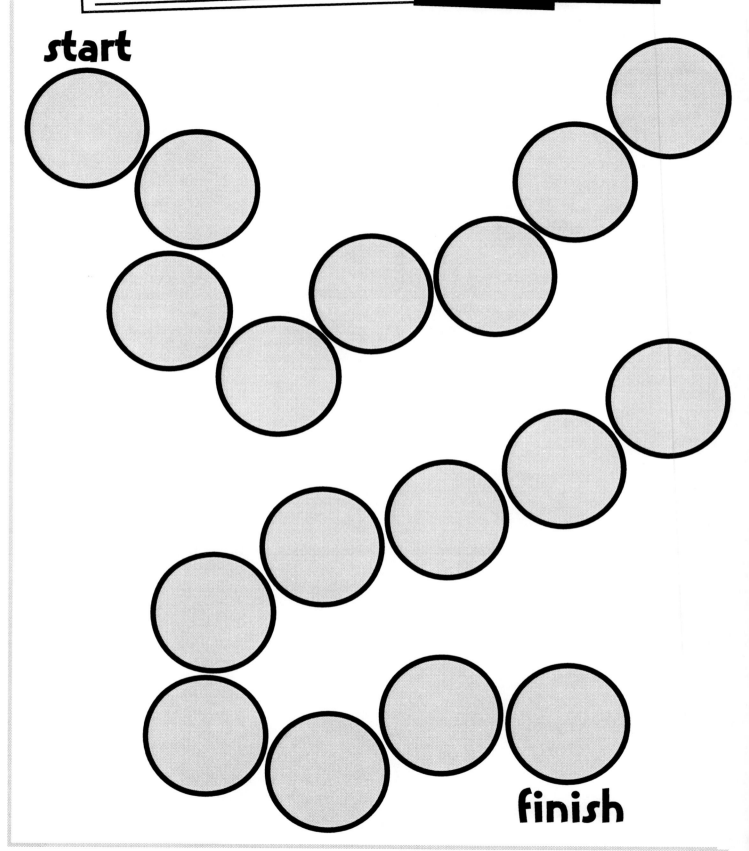

_____'s BOARD GAME

start

finish

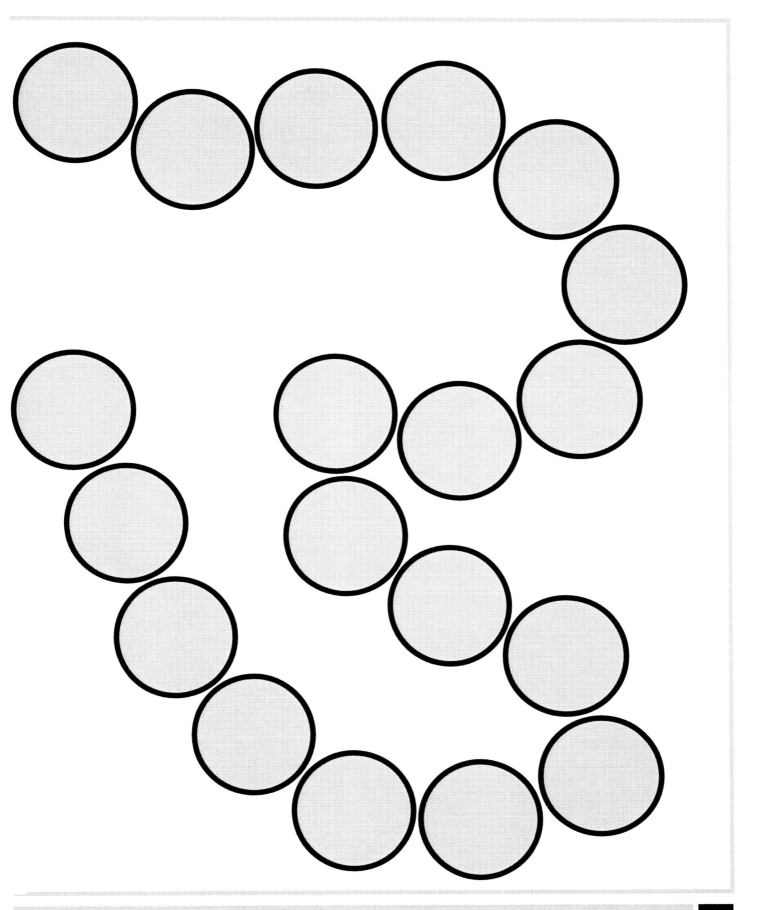

ANIMAL MIXOLOGY

Use these animal body parts to invent a new animal.

ANIMAL MIXOLOGY

SUPER SHOPPING SPREE

Look through magazines, flyers or catalogues and go shopping! Cut out the picture and draw or paste the combination of coins needed to buy the item.

A HEALTHY MEAL

Draw a healthy meal onto the plate. Label the food.

Why is your meal healthy?

_____

_____

_____

MORE TIME FILLER IDEAS

1. Poem of the Day

Have students keep an anthology of their favourite poems. Students can copy their poems into a special notebook and illustrate them. This is also a good opportunity for students to practice their penmanship. Keep a sign up sheet for poetry readings so when there is extra time in class students will be prepared to read their favourite poetry.

2. Daily Physical Exercise

Take a few minutes as a class and do some kind of physical activity. It can be anything from a stretch to challenging students to see how many jumping jacks, pushups etc they can do in one minute. Students also enjoy doing aerobics to music.

3. Classroom Cleanup

Challenge students to pick up, straighten, or put away 100 things in the classroom in 100 seconds.

4. Broken Telephone

Broken telephone is a fantastic game that students never tire of in which each successive student whispers to the next a phrase or sentence whispered to them by the preceding student. As the message is communicated, cumulative errors from mishearing often happen and consequently the sentence heard by the last player is completely different.

5. Nonsense Words

Reading pronounceable nonsense words is a great way for students to practice their decoding skills. Create nonsense words with a combination of blends, short or long vowels, consonant digraphs and diphthongs. For example: claphenomologicalide

6. Board Games

Have a supply of games on hand for students to play such asSnakes and Ladders or Scrabble. Challenge students to create their own version of their favourite game using the board game black line master found in this resource as a guide.

7. Top Ten List

Create a top ten list as a whole class. Topics can include; people they admire, favourite movies, etc.

8. Daily Math Problems

Challenge students to create math problems for members of the class to solve based on what math concept is being currently studied. Have students write the math problems on index cards with the solution on the back so that they are easily on hand.

MORE TIME FILLER IDEAS

9. Dictionary Game

Expand students' vocabulary with this fun challenge. Read out a word and have students race to find the meaning of the word in the dictionary. Then have students try to use the word in a sentence. This challenge also works well using a subject related glossary.

10. Joke or Riddle of the Day

Keep a list of jokes and riddle books handy to share with the class.

11. Class Messages

Class Messages are an excellent way to provide students with interesting facts about the theme they are studying while also arranging teachable moments in the use of grammar and punctuation. Write a class message in a letter format with grammatical and punctuation errors. Then have students help you edit the message. Once completely edited, use the class message as a springboard for a class discussion.

12. Alphabet Challenge

Challenge students to name a proper noun for each letter of the alphabet. Other examples of alphabet challenges include verbs, foods, cities, or names.

13. Animal Mixology

Have students create a new animal by mixing and matching the features of several of the animals using the black line masters in this book or their own ideas. For instance, a student might combine the ears of a bunny with a giraffe's neck, a dog's body, and a lion's tail! Encourage students to name their animals, to describe their habitat and other interesting facts.

14. Create a Class Store

A class store is a great way for older students to practice their math within a "real world" context. Students have an opportunity to gain experience with multiplication, addition, subtraction, decimals, multiplication and division. Encourage students to bring in different packages, empty products, menus or store flyers for the students to "buy" in the store. Label and price items using stickers or index cards. Assign students as customers who will "buy" items from the store and students who will act as cashiers who "sell" in the store. Before customers go shopping give them a set amount of money to spend. Use notebooks to keep track of purchases and change.

MORE TIME FILLER IDEAS

15. Analogy Puzzles

Challenge students to create analogy puzzles to keep on hand when you have a few minutes to fill. Analogies are a fantastic tool for stimulating students to think critically. Write examples of a few analogies on the chalkboard and challenge students to come up with the appropriate conclusion to each analogy. For example; German Shepard is to dog as Cardinal is to_____. Have students share their responses and the reasoning behind them. Once students have the ideas of how an analogy works challenge students to create their own.

16. Math Race

Reinforce important math skills. Challenge students to list numbers with specific attributes, math facts, multiples of numbers or to continue number patterns within a one minute time frame. Students can compete two a time at the chalkboard.

17. Hangman

Hangman is always a popular game with students. Try a twist to the traditional hangman game by using words related to a specific subject, time period, or famous Canadians. For example, play the game using words related to Canada. Those words might include names of provinces or famous Canadian landmarks.

18. What Did We Learn in School Today?

Keep parents informed about class happenings with this easy weekly newsletter! Take a few minutes at the end of each school day and ask students what they learned in school. Record each comment in the appropriate day of the week box on the blackline master found in this book. The teacher may wish to also record a student's initials after each comment. Use the notes box to recommend a website or to remind parents about important information.

19. Share Personal Happenings

Have students share personal happenings in their lives.

20. Learning Logs

Have students keep a learning log to fill out whenever they have some spare time. This is not only a time filler, but is an effective way for a teacher to gain insight as to what a student has learned or is thinking about. Learning logs can include the following:

- teacher prompts
- student personal reflections
- questions that arise
- connections discovered
- labeled diagrams and pictures

WEBSITES FOR KIDS

Encourage students to visit interesting and age appropriate websites.

Yahooligans! • www.yahooligans.com

This site is based on the popular adult Yahoo! Site. It's an excellent and safe place for students to look for information and has an extensive list of age-appropriate reference links.

Ask Jeeves Kids • www.ajkids.com

This is a fantastic search engine where kids can ask questions that interest them.

How Stuff Works • www.howstuffworks.com

This is an award-winning site that tells kids how different things work and answers interesting questions such as: Does gum really stay in you for seven years?

Recycle City • www.epa.gov/recyclecity/

This is a great interactive website for students to learn about recycling at Recycle City. Students will find out what happens to garbage and why recycling is important. The site Includes a game and other activities.

Kids Reads • www.kidsreads.com

This is a great website for students to find information about their favourite books and authors, including excerpts from the hottest new releases.

Mister Rogers Neighbourhood • http://pbskids.org/rogers/

The Mister Rogers Neighourhood website has sections where kids can build their own neighbourhood or take a factory tour to see how things are made.

School Net • www.schoolnet.ca

This Government of Canada site has more than 7,000 links for kids and parents on a variety of news-related topics across Canada. It's great for school projects, since all federal resource sites are listed in one place.

Science Made Simple • www.sciencemadesimple.com

This is a terrific site for students to learn science . Explanations are presented in an easy, hands-on way with clear, detailed answers. There are also tonnes of fun projects and experiments.

AAA math • www.aaamath.com

AAA Math is a first-rate math website that features a comprehensive set of interactive arithmetic lessons. Students can have unlimited practice on any math topic which allows thorough reinforcement and mastery of math concepts.

National Geographic Kids! • www.nationalgeographic.com/kids/index.html

This website allows students to read about current affairs in easy-to-understand language. Students will enjoy learning about new archaeological digs and historical discoveries.

I Know That • www.iknowthat.com

This website is always a favourite and provides students with stimulating educational games and activities. Activities include stickerbooks, simulation games, painting, math and phonics. Students will especially enjoy playing Leon math adventures!